Please Don't Leave Me!

By

Vic Sbarbaro
Marcia Sbarbaro - Pezzella

Illustrated by Josh Smith

Northstate Children's Books

Please Don't Leave Me

By Vic Sbarbaro and Marcia Sbarbaro-Pezzella

© 2014 Vic Sbarbaro. All rights reserved.
No part of this book may be reproduced without permission.

Printed in the United States of America

ISBN: 9780982876756

Library of Congress Control Number: 2014913950

Published by:
NORTH STATE CHILDREN'S BOOKS

Marcia D. Sbarbaro - Pezzella was born and raised in Weed, California, (Siskiyou County), 68 years ago. She has always had compassion and concerns for the underdog and because of this has worked as a probation officer, an employee of Napa State Hospital, and a special education teacher for disabled children for 35 years in San Lorenzo, California. She has also had a career in the entertainment field for 45 years. She has since retired and helps out in her husband's restaurant, Pezzella's. She is proud to be an American and equally proud to be Italian. She is devoted to her family and many friends.

Vic Sbarbaro, EdD, CHES, is an instructor at California State University, Chico, and Butte Community College. He is a Certified Health Education Specialist (CHES) who specializes in health education for elementary school teachers, multicultural education issues, emergency care and aquatic safety. He works continuously through the American Red Cross, Three Rivers Chapter, Butte County Branch as an instructor and instructor trainer. He also instructs Adapted Aquatics in the summer time, and works with middle school students through a Summer Connection Program at Butte Community College.

Josh Smith graduated from CSU, Chico. He is currently a freelance painter and illustrator. He majored in Communication Design.

DEDICATION

To those who have been left behind, but have a special mission in life.

Chapter 1

There was a small town called Leafton with a population that included about 500 people. The families in the small community were struggling with their businesses due to the floods and fires throughout the previous year. One of the families that lived in the community was the Thompsons, who lived in a small cottage with a big backyard full of many kinds of trees that included oak, ash, elm, and evergreen to name a few. Towards the back of the yard stood a magnificent maple tree with barren branches from the last days of winter.

It was a beautiful morning on March 21, the first day of spring. New tree and flower shoots were beginning to appear. The new leaves and flower buds began to form and take on various shapes and sizes. As the March winds whistled through the trees, the leaves began to rustle and shimmer. If you listened closely it sounded like idle chatter and conversations going on amongst all of the plants, flowers and leaves.

Two weeks had passed and then a tiny shoot from the maple tree began to sprout. One very small leaf began to form and take shape. Hey! "How did all of the leaves get so high on the branches?"

All of the other plants, leaves, and flowers were friends and they all had names: Daffy the daffodil, Tula the tulip, Levi the lavender bush, Rosita the rose, Ashley the ash tree, Zack the zucchini plant, Lila the lilac bush, Gerry the geranium, Delbert the dogwood tree, …and each leaf had a name.

As all of the other leaves were frolicking high in the air the branches began to sway back and forth. The one little leaf still noticed that he was lower on the tree than all of the other leaves, but wanted to grow faster so that he too could be on a branch that was high in the air with all of his friends.

The little leaf would feel confused because everyone had a real name but him. All of the other leaves would call him nicknames: "leafy", "little buddy", "small fry", or "runt". All of the other leaves looked after the little leaf who was very happy – go – lucky and made friends easily. The leaves told him that one day he would have a special name because he had an important mission in life. The little leaf wondered, "what is my mission in life going to be?"

The weather started to turn hot and it was the beginning of summer. Each morning Mr. Thompson would go outside to water the plants, flowers, and trees. The little leaf would look forward to this because he would be so thirsty, excited, and noticed that he was starting to get bigger like all of the other leaves. During the summer rains the little leaf would shout out to his friends Yippee! It is raining, Live, Laugh, and Love each other. "LET A SMILE BE YOUR UMBRELLA ON A RAINY DAY".

Chapter 2

The summer months had come and gone and autumn was in the air. The days began to get cooler and shorter with less sunlight. All of the leaves began to turn into the most magnificent colors of bright red, yellow, orange, and gold. As the days continued on, the little leaf noticed that all of the leaves on the higher branches were starting to change colors into a rustic tan and light brown. The little leaf was still displaying all of his very bright and vibrant colors.

The northern winds came along and were howling like the wolves. The leaves were being blown all over the back yard. The little leaf started to feel sad and began shouting at the top of his voice, "PLEASE DON'T LEAVE ME!" All of the other fallen leaves were yelling back "see you later leafy", "bye small fry", "hurry and come and join us – little buddy." The little leaf started to feel lonely and decided to sing a couple of songs: "Blowing in the Wind" and "Please Don't Leave Me this Way".

Chapter 3

It was the day before Thanksgiving and there were many chores that needed to be completed at the Thompson home. The Thompsons were inviting several neighbors over to the Thanksgiving feast. Many of their neighbors had lost their homes and many personal items in the floods and fires.

Ms. Thompson and her daughter, Anna, went into town to shop for some table decorations for the holiday. They put the decorations in the car and then went into the grocery store to buy a turkey and the "fixings" for the big feast the next day. As Ms. Thompson and Anna came out of the grocery store, they noticed that the car was unlocked and someone had taken all of the Thanksgiving table decorations. The little girl, Anna, felt very sad because there would be no table centerpiece decoration to share with the family and neighbors.

When Ms. Thompson and Anna arrived back home, Mr. Thompson was busily raking up all of the leaves. He notices that there was one leaf left on the maple tree and then goes over to cut it down. "Wait!" Anna yells out to her father, "please Dad, LEAVE ON that last leaf of the maple tree, it looks like a miracle leaf because of its shape and array of bright colors."

The little leaf finally decided that must be my name, **LEAVE ON**! I like my name. I must be special because I have two parts to my name, Leave and On and I am still the only leaf left on the tree.

It was the night before Thanksgiving and a big gust of wind came along and LEAVE ON gently fell to the ground.

Chapter 4

The little girl, Anna, went outside on Thanksgiving morning to play with Rosco, the family dog. Anna noticed the miracle leaf with all of the beautiful colors intact lying on the ground. Anna then had a bright idea. She would pick up the leaf and use it for the table centerpiece for the Thanksgiving dinner. As she picked up the colorful leaf she noticed that the leaf appeared to have a smiling face. LEAVE ON thought to himself, all of my friends were right because they told me that I had a special mission in life!

Before dinner, the family said grace and everyone shared what they were thankful for. Anna was last to share her thoughts and graciously said that she was thankful for this miracle leaf that was used for the table centerpiece decoration. Anna honestly believed that the special leaf had brightened up everyone's spirits on this wonderful day.

After the Thanksgiving dinner, Anna put the miracle leaf in her keep sake, scrap book, photo album. She then would spray the leaf with a special varnish so that the leaf would keep its shape and color for a long time.

Many years have come and gone and Anna is now an elderly woman. Anna gets out her keep sake, scrap book, photo album every Thanksgiving and fondly tells her children and grandchildren one of her favorite stories about the miracle leaf and how it was used for the table centerpiece decoration that brightened up everyone's spirits.

CPSIA information can be obtained
at www.ICGtesting.com
Printed in the USA
LVRC022103250119
605314LV00001B/8